Specials!

Native American Indians

Nichola Boughey

Acknowledgements

© 2008 Folens Limited, on behalf of the author.

United Kingdom: Folens Publishers, Waterslade House, Thame Road, Haddenham, Buckinghamshire, HP17 8NT.
Email: info@folens.com

Ireland: Folens Publishers, Greenhills Road, Tallaght, Dublin 24.
Email: info@folens.ie

Folens allows photocopying of pages marked 'copiable page' for educational use, providing that this use is within the confines of the purchasing institution. Copiable pages should not be declared in any return in respect of any photocopying licence.

Folens publications are protected by international copyright laws. All rights are reserved. The copyright of all materials in this publication, except where otherwise stated, remains the property of the publisher and the author. No part of this publication may be reproduced, stored in a retrieval system, or transmitted, in any form or by any means, for whatever purpose, without the written permission of Folens Limited.

Nichola Boughey hereby asserts her moral right to be identified as the author of this work in accordance with the Copyright, Designs and Patents Act 1988.

Editor: Kayleigh Buller

Cover design: Martin Cross

Illustrations: Neil Sutton, Pumpkin House

Layout artist: Planman Technologies

Cover image: Kansas State Historical Society

First published 2008 by Folens Limited.

Every effort has been made to contact copyright holders of material used in this publication. If any copyright holder has been overlooked, we should be pleased to make any necessary arrangements.

British Library Cataloguing in Publication Data. A catalogue record for this publication is available from the British Library.

ISBN 978-1-85008-369-6

Contents

Introduction	4
The First Arrivals	5
Native American keywords	6
Map-How did people travel to America?	7
New settlers arrive	8
New settlers arrive activities	9
Assessment sheet	10
The Plains Indians	11
The Plains Indians	12
An Indian tepee	13
Design a tepee	14
The Sioux wordsearch	15
Assessment sheet	16
Native American Customs	17
What was daily life like for a Sioux Indian?	18
Nippiwan's diary (part one)	19
Nippiwan's diary (part two)	20
Everyday life	21
Sioux children	22
History bingo	23
Assessment sheet	24
The Buffalo	25
A world before shops	26
The buffalo hunt	27
The buffalo	28
What was the buffalo used for?	29
One-stop shop	30
Assessment sheet	31
Marriage and Divorce	32
Why do we get married?	33
Sioux marriages	34
Polygamy	35
Polygamous marriage	36
Sioux divorce	37
Assessment sheet	38

Native American Beliefs	39
What was the Great Spirit?	40
Sioux religion	41
Wakan Tanka	42
The Medicine Man	43
Medicine Man advert	44
Assessment sheet	45
Native American Warfare	46
Why did Sioux Indians fight?	47
Bravery in battle	48
Bravery in battle activities	49
An account of a battle	50
Assessment sheet	51
Problems with White Settlers	52
Settlers arrive	53
Settlers arrive source sheet	54
Settlers arrive worksheet	55
Settlers arrive essay task	56
Assessment sheet	57
Battle of Little Big Horn	58
Who would win?	59
Battle of Little Big Horn (1)	60
Battle of Little Big Horn (2)	61
Warrior diary	62
Newspaper report	63
Assessment sheet	64

Introduction

Specials! *History* have been specifically written for teachers to use with students who may struggle with some of the skills and concepts needed for Key Stage 3 History. The titles are part of a wider series from Folens for use with lower ability students.

Each book in the series contains ten separate units covering the topics needed to complete the theme of the book. Each unit has one or more photocopiable Resource sheets and several Activity sheets. This allows the teacher to work in different ways. The tasks are differentiated throughout the book and offer all students the opportunity to expand their skills. By using photocopiable writing frames and emphasising literacy skills, students will be able to access historical information more easily.

The Teacher's notes give guidance and are laid out as follows:

Objectives
These are the main skills or knowledge to be learned.

Prior knowledge
This refers to the minimum skills or knowledge required by the students to complete the tasks. As a rule, students should have a reading comprehension age of 7 to 10 years and should be working at levels 2 to 4. Some Activity sheets are more challenging than others and you will need to select accordingly.

QCA and NC links
The 2008 teaching themes fit into a number of different areas, which are not clarified at time of going to press.

Background
This provides additional information for the teacher, expanding on historical details or giving further information about this unit.

Starter activity
Since the units can be taught as a lesson, a warm-up activity focusing on an aspect of the unit is suggested.

Resource sheets and Activity sheets
The Resource sheets, which are often visual but may also be written, do not include tasks and can be used as stimulus for discussion. Related tasks are provided on Activity sheets. Where necessary, keywords are included on the student pages. Other keywords are included on the Teacher's notes pages. These can be introduced to students at the teacher's discretion and depending on the students' ability.

Plenary
The teacher can use the suggestions here to recap on the main points covered or to reinforce a particular idea. Look out for other titles in the History series, which include:
- *Specials! History* The Tudors
- *Specials! History* The Norman Conquest

Assessment sheet
At the end of each chapter, is an assessment sheet focusing on student progress. They can be used in different ways. A student can complete it as a self-assessment, while the teacher also completes one on each student's progress. They can then compare the two. This is useful in situations where the teacher or classroom assistant is working with one student. Alternatively, students can work in pairs to carry out peer assessments and then compare the outcomes with each other. Starting from a simple base that students can manage, the assessment sheet allows the student to discuss their own progress, to consider different points of view and to discuss how they might improve, thus enabling the teacher to see the work from the students perspective.

Teacher's notes

The First Arrivals

Objectives

- To develop a knowledge of Native American keywords
- To understand how the first settlers arrived in America
- To understand what nomads were

Prior knowledge

Students should be aware of how the history of other countries has an impact upon other cultures.

QCA and NC links

Understand the diverse experience and ideas, beliefs and attitudes of men, women and children in past societies and how these have shaped the world.

Northern Ireland PoS

Identify and analyse the characteristic features of periods and societies studied.

Scottish attainment targets

Describe the diversity of lifestyles of people in the past.

Resource sheets and Activity sheets

Read through Resource sheet, 'Native American keywords', with the students and clarify as a group what each of the words means with reference to modern day examples if possible.

In Resource sheet, 'Map-How did people travel to America?', students will look at this map and use it to help develop the next activity.

The Resource sheet, 'New settlers arrive', explains to students how and why the first settlers travelled from Asia to America using both text and diagrams. The information from this sheet will be needed to complete the Activity sheet that follows.

'New settlers arrive activities', includes activities which require students to read written information to form their answers. It may be useful for a teacher to read through the second activity with the class before allowing them to complete it by themselves.

Plenary

Students should play keyword bingo based upon all of the new words learnt during this unit.

Assessment sheet

Students should complete the tick sheet at the end of this unit.

Background

Students will need to be made aware that the first settlers to arrive in America walked across a land bridge that attached Asia to America at the Bering Strait. Once they arrived in America they followed their food supply, buffalos, in a nomadic way but when they returned to the land bridge it was underwater and thus they became the first settlers in America.

Starter activity

Ask students to brainstorm, on the board, all of the different ways that a person can travel to America. Once you have a list draw out from the class the pros and cons of each method of travel.

Resource sheet – The First Arrivals

Native american keywords

The first humans on planet earth came from Africa. These humans travelled from Africa all over the rest of the world.

How did these people travel to America?

Today people from Europe and Asia can only travel to North and South America by boat or plane. However, thousands of years ago people travelled from Asia to America on foot. They travelled across a land bridge at the Bering Strait. Over the next 1000 years these people would settle across all of America.

You will be introduced to new keywords about Native Americans throughout this book. Have a look at some of them below:

Keywords	Definitions
Nomadic	Somebody who moves from place to place
Buffalo	An animal that was used for food and tools
Tribe	A large group of people who lived together
Divorce	When a husband and wife split up
Wakan Tanka	The Native American God
Polygamy	Having more than one wife
Counting Coup	Touching an enemy in battle
Scalp	The part of your head that has hair
Tepee	A large tent that people live in
Exposure	Leaving a person behind when they get old

Resource sheet – The First Arrivals

Map – How did people travel to America?

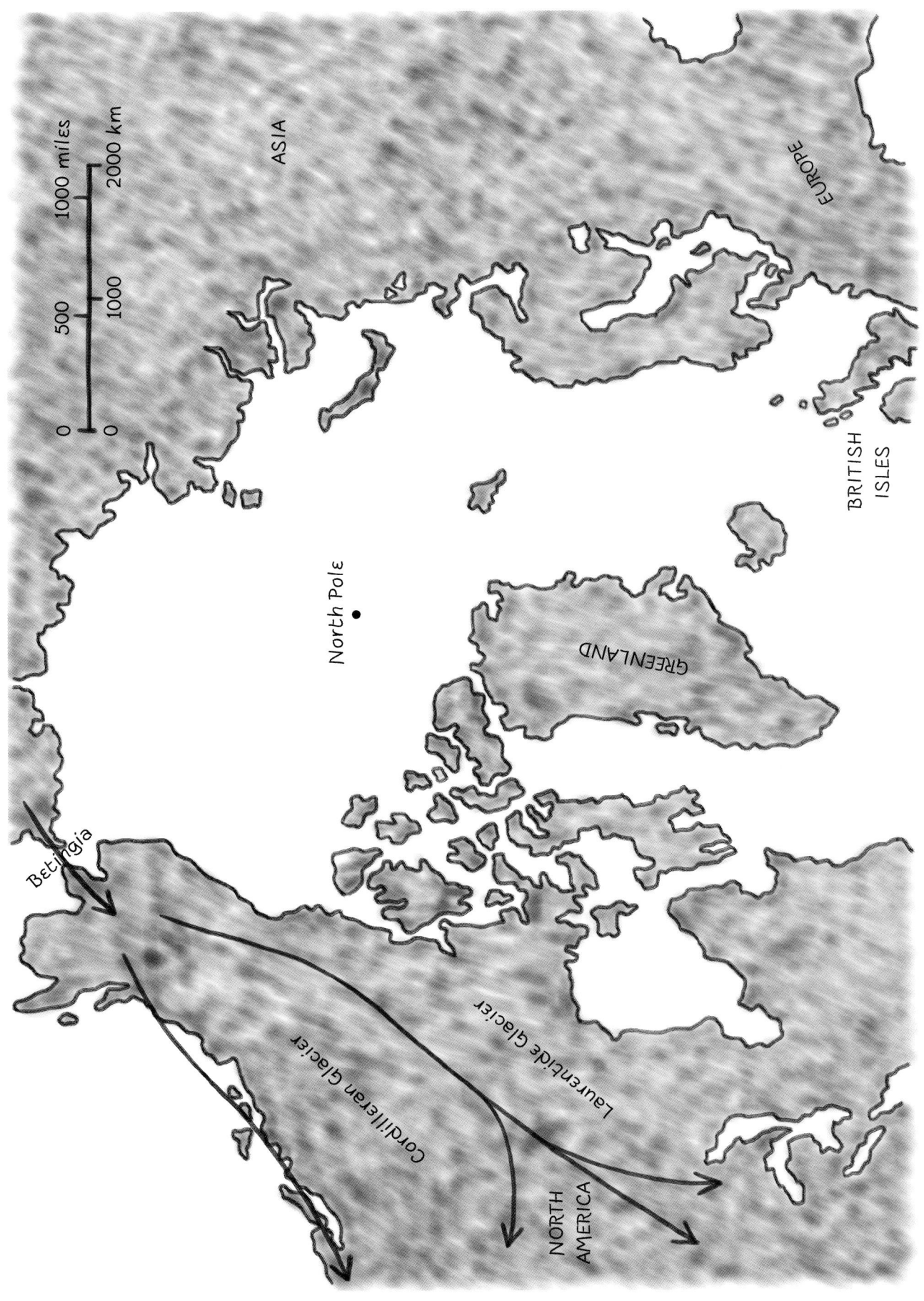

Resource sheet – The First Arrivals

New settlers arrive

The first people walked to America from Asia across a land bridge at the Bering Strait. They were nomads. These nomads did not live in one place and followed animals that they hunted for food. They also needed new land where they could pick fruit and berries. If you look at the Resource sheet, 'Map – How did people travel to America?', you can see the route that many of these Indians followed when they walked to America.

About 11000 years ago the new settlers spread out across both South and North America. Today we call them Native American Indians. Native American tribes were not all the same.

Each tribe had their own language and historians believe that they had over 2000 different languages. Native American Indians did not read or write so they passed all of their history and knowledge on through stories.

The earliest information that historians have about Indian tribes comes from the first white European settlers in America. This information is not always positive because the settlers did not understand the language or traditions of the natives and this made them dislike the Native American Indians.

They did not speak the same language

Some lived by the sea

Some lived in forests

How were Native American tribes different?

Some fished for food

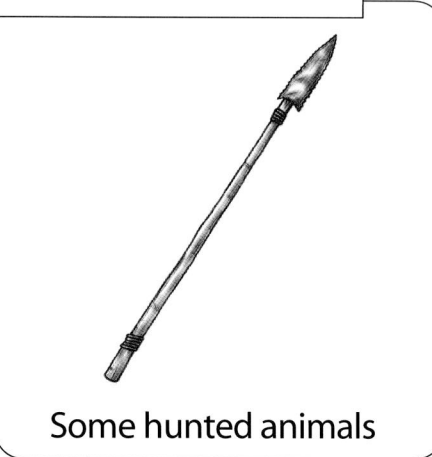
Some hunted animals

8   Native American Indians   © Folens (copiable page)

Activity sheet – The First Arrivals

New settlers arrive activities

Use the information from the Resource sheets in this section to complete the activities below.

☞ 1 Read through the paragraph below. Using the Resource sheet, 'New Settlers Arrive', fill in the blank spaces.

   The first people to walk to America came from _____. They walked across a _____ bridge. It took _____ years for these nomads to spread out across America. The first settlers _____ for food and needed new _____ for fruit and berries.

☞ 2 Work with a partner to make a list, in the box below, of all the ways that Native American Tribes were different. The first one has been completed for you.

How were Native American Indian tribes different?
• *They did not speak the same language.*

© Folens (copiable page)   Native American Indians   9

Assessment sheet – The First Arrivals

✓ Tick the boxes to show what you know.

I know:

	Yes	Not sure	Don't know
what nomad means			
what Native American Indian means			
what a land bridge was			
what type of food the Natives ate			
how to select information			
how to use text to create a list			
how to use information to complete tasks			

The thing that I remember the most about this unit is:

_____

_____

_____

_____

_____

Teacher's notes

The Plains Indians

Objectives

- To understand where the Plains Indians lived
- To understand the lifestyle of the Sioux Indians
- To use written information to complete visual tasks

Prior knowledge

Students will be aware of how the first settlers travelled across the Bering land bridge from Asia to America and then spread out across to live in different parts of their new country.

QCA and NC links

Identify and investigate, individually and as part of a team, specific historical questions or issues, making and testing hypotheses.

Northern Ireland PoS

Describe and explain important historical concepts associated with the periods studied.

Scottish attainment targets

Describe the diversity of lifestyles of people in the past.

Resource sheets and Activity sheets

The Resource sheet, 'The Plains Indians', will provide students with an overview of who the Sioux Indians were and the type of lifestyle that they had.

Resource sheet, 'An Indian tepee', follows on from the previous sheet by exploring the way that the Native American Indians lived. It focuses on the importance of the tepee.

Activity sheet, 'Design a tepee', asks students to consider what items they deem important to them and then asks them to draw these items inside of the tepee template that is provided for them.

Plenary

The students should complete a wordsearch on the Sioux Indians as provided in this unit.

Assessment sheet

Students should complete a true or false set of activity to assess what they have learned during this unit of the textbook.

Background

The new settlers spread out across America. Some of these Native American Indians chose to live by the sea and fish for food. Some decided to live on the Great Plains and grasslands of America. They had a nomadic lifestyle and followed their main source of food. The largest Plains tribe were the Sioux or Lakota Indians.

Starter activity

Students should brainstorm on the board as to what type of 'housing' they think Native American Indians lived in.

Resource sheet – The Plains Indians

The Plains Indians

The Plains Indians were the largest group of Native American Indians that lived in America. They lived on the Great Plains in the middle of the country. These are sometimes called the grasslands of America because they are covered in grass.

The biggest tribe living on the Great Plains was called the Sioux or Lakota Indians. This tribe of Indians did not live in one place but travelled around the Great Plains following their main food supply – buffalos.

The Sioux tribe originally lived in the East Woodlands of America but later moved to the Great Plains.

Tribes who did not stay in one place all year round were called nomads. The Sioux Indians would move their camps at least three times every year, following the buffalo. This meant that they could not live in houses and lived in tents instead. These tents were called tepees.

Tepees were like big tents with poles covered in buffalo skin and decorated with paintings of items that were important to the family that lived in them. These tepees were quick and easy for Native Americans to put up and take down. Sioux Indians used horses to drag these tepees around the Great Plains.

Resource sheet – The Plains Indians

An Indian tepee

The tepee was very important to Sioux Indians. It was a place to live, a place to cook and a place to raise a family. Most importantly, it was a place to store all of the items that a Native American Indian family needed to live.

Sioux tepees were decorated inside with hand-drawn pictures and handmade wooden chests containing warriors' weapons and food.

Sioux families would build a fire inside of the tepee where they could cook their food and keep their tepee warm during the winter.

The inside of the tepee was also decorated with buffalo skins, which were used as carpets. Buffalo skins were also placed as blankets on the top of wooden beds.

Sioux men had many jobs and were responsible for hunting the buffalo, providing food and keeping their family and tribe safe. Sioux women cooked family meals as well as making clothes. They took care of their children and were also responsible for packing up the tepee whenever it was time to move camp. A skilled wife could pack the tepee up in just 15 minutes.

☞ Use the Resource sheet from, 'The Plains Indians', to complete the questions below. Use a separate piece of paper for your answers.

1 Where did most Indians live?

2 What was the name of the largest tribe living on the Great Plains?

3 What does the word, nomadic, mean?

4 Read through the information again and explain in your own words why you think that Sioux Indians found it easier to live in tepees.

Activity sheet – The Plains Indians

Design a tepee

Sioux women were given the job of making tepees. They were hard to make and women who made them were very skilled. They would soften and then sew together between 18–20 buffalo skins to make a tepee.

Tepees were very important to the Sioux Indians. They kept all of their important belongings inside them.

☞ Drawn below is the inside of a tepee. You must draw all of the things that are important to you inside it. Make sure that you label them and colour them in.

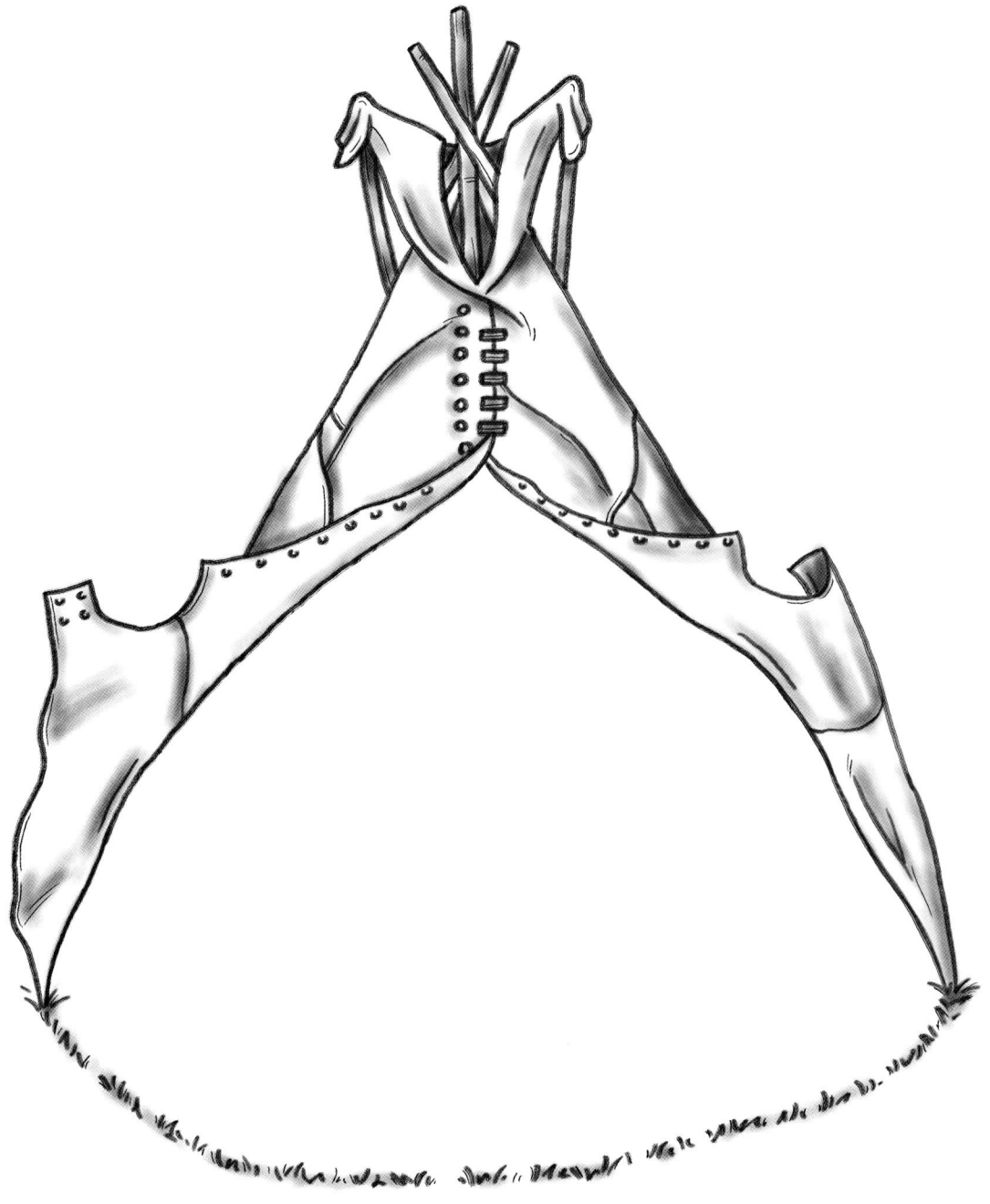

Activity sheet – The Plains Indians

The Sioux Wordsearch

☞ Find the words below in the wordsearch.

AMERICA	HORSES	NOMAD	TENT
WARRIORS	BUFFALO	INDIANS	PLAINS
TEPEE	WOMEN	GREAT	MEN
SIOUX	TRIBE		

The words will appear either across or down.

S	N	A	L	O	R	T	A	D	A	B	T	X	I	U	H	S
X	G	V	H	P	G	M	G	R	E	A	T	N	A	F	W	M
F	F	O	S	L	R	L	A	F	T	D	O	N	B	K	O	X
F	N	L	V	A	R	T	E	P	E	E	J	I	S	X	M	I
G	L	S	F	I	I	A	I	W	N	E	E	O	O	Q	E	P
G	J	E	V	N	O	M	A	D	T	C	D	U	M	E	N	D
T	R	J	N	S	Y	E	T	O	Z	N	Z	V	U	G	O	B
V	B	A	A	I	U	R	M	I	M	A	H	A	T	P	L	X
L	U	I	Z	O	T	I	P	E	V	R	O	B	E	U	D	G
R	F	L	T	S	F	C	I	W	A	R	R	I	O	R	S	L
B	F	F	N	C	S	A	N	F	X	T	S	V	S	B	S	D
A	A	O	P	Y	L	R	D	E	S	S	E	Z	I	V	V	U
T	L	T	M	E	N	O	I	U	T	I	S	I	O	U	X	D
S	O	E	Z	T	L	O	A	I	S	L	E	F	O	P	D	P
T	P	Y	D	R	N	U	N	O	C	T	R	I	B	E	H	J
O	Y	L	S	D	V	S	S	H	L	R	D	U	K	V	X	Z
T	Y	M	Y	S	C	F	R	Z	R	H	N	R	U	B	E	I

Assessment sheet – The Plains Indians

Use this sheet to see how much you can remember about the Sioux Indians and their tepees.

✓ Tick the ones that are true.

X Cross the ones that are false.

	The Sioux Indians stayed in one place all year.

The Sioux Indians were nomads.	

	The Sioux Indians followed wolves across the Great Plains.

The Sioux Indians lived in caravans.	

	The Sioux Indians decorated their tepees with pictures that were important to them.

Women did no work in the Sioux camps.	

	The warriors hunted buffalo.

Tepees were made out of 100–120 buffalo skins.	

Teacher's notes

Native American Customs

Objectives

- To understand what life was like in a Sioux camp
- Appreciate how different members of the Sioux tribe were treated
- To learn how to make decisions

Prior knowledge

Students should be aware of the fact that Native Americans lived in nomadic camps rather than houses so their lifestyle and customs were very different for men, women and children.

QCA and NC links

Present and organise accounts and explanations about the past that are coherent, structured and substantiated, using chronological conventions and historical vocabulary.

Northern Ireland PoS

Recalling, select and organise information deploying terms accurately to communicate their knowledge and understanding of history.

Scottish attainment targets

Describe the diversity of lifestyles of people in the past.

Background

The nomadic nature and lifestyle of the Sioux tribe meant that their attitudes towards tribe laws, marriage, children and family life were very different to ours today. Native Americans worked together for the good of the tribe and made sure that all boys and girls were raised to either be good hunters or wives, by learning from their parents.

Starter activity

The teacher writes a sentence on the board which reflects the topic being studied and students have to find other keywords from the letters in the sentence.

Resource sheets and Activity sheets

The Resource sheet, 'What was daily life like for a Sioux Indian?', provides students with information about everyday life for Sioux Indians when they were camped on the Great Plains.

As a class read through 'Nippiwan's diary, (part one) and (part two)'. Try and draw out from the class all of the differences between life today and life in a Sioux Camp.

The Activity sheet, 'Everyday life', asks students to use information from 'Nippiwan's diary' to complete a selection task and a decision making activity.

Plenary sheet

Finally, students will use Activity sheet, 'History bingo', to complete a game of bingo using all of the keywords from this unit.

Plenary

The teacher can play a game of 'Three in a row before you can go'. The teacher thinks of questions relevant to the ability of the group and the students have to answer three in a row correctly before they can leave the classroom.

Assessment sheet

Students should complete the tick sheet at the end of this unit.

Resource sheet – Native American Customs

What was daily life like for a Sioux Indian?

The Sioux Indians believed in a strong sense of community. Everybody in the tribe had a job to do:

- Men hunted for food and defended the camp when they needed to.
- Women cooked, cleaned and looked after the family.
- Children were expected to help their parents with work.

Sioux Indians who were too old to hunt or fight were often asked to sit on a council, which made important decisions about the camp, such as punishing people who had broken Sioux rules and deciding if the camp should go to war.

A camp was always busy as there were plenty of jobs to be done. The picture above shows many different activities that took place in a Sioux Indian camp.

Resource sheet – Native American Customs

Nippiwan's diary (part one)

Every day was different in a Sioux camp. Below are some diary extracts written by Nippiwan. She was a young Sioux Indian girl who will help you to learn all about the Sioux way of life.

Everybody was excited in camp today. The wise and respected men in the tribe held a Sioux Council to try and decide if we should go to war with the tribe that keeps stealing our horses. I loved seeing them dressed up in ceremonial clothes. My dad is keen to fight the enemy and has been practicing with his bow and arrow all day.

I tripped my brother up today. My mother was so angry that she threw a bucket of water over me and told me that I can't help her with the cooking or play with my doll!

My brother was really naughty today. I never see dad shout at him but he has stopped him from playing war games with his friends and going hunting. This has never happened before.

Resource sheet – Native American Customs

Nippiwan's diary (part two)

I have spent the whole day crying. I had to help my mother pack up the tepee today because we are moving camp again. My grandmother has been sick for a while and she could not help us pack the tepee away. I heard my dad talking to mum about leaving her behind because she is too old to help the tribe anymore. I have seen this happen to lots of families before and grandmother is not upset about being left behind. I am going to miss her.

My dad is getting married again this afternoon. He keeps killing more buffalo than any other hunters and this means that he needs more wives to clean them. He has chosen a new wife who will join our family. I like her because she is pretty and works really hard around the camp.

Activity sheet – Native American Customs

Everyday life

Use this sheet to help you to remember the most important details about life in a Sioux Indian camp.

 1 Cross out the wrong words in the passage below to the make sentences read correctly.

Nippiwan was a **Sioux/British** Indian; her family lived on the Great Plains of **America/Asia**. They lived in a **bungalow/tepee**. During the day, women **hunted/cooked** and men **fought/cooked** with enemy tribes. Most of the big decisions were made by the **oldest/youngest** members of the tribe, who sat on the Sioux Council. When Nippiwan's father killed the most buffalo he was allowed to take more **wives/money**. This was called polygamy, which means a man having more than one **wife/tepee**. Nippiwan was very upset because her grandmother was too **old/young** to travel with the rest of the tribe when they moved camp, so she was left behind. This was called exposure and **did not/did** happen very often.

 2 Now, read through 'Nippiwan's diary' again. Choose four facts about life in a Sioux camp and write them down in the boxes on the diagram below.

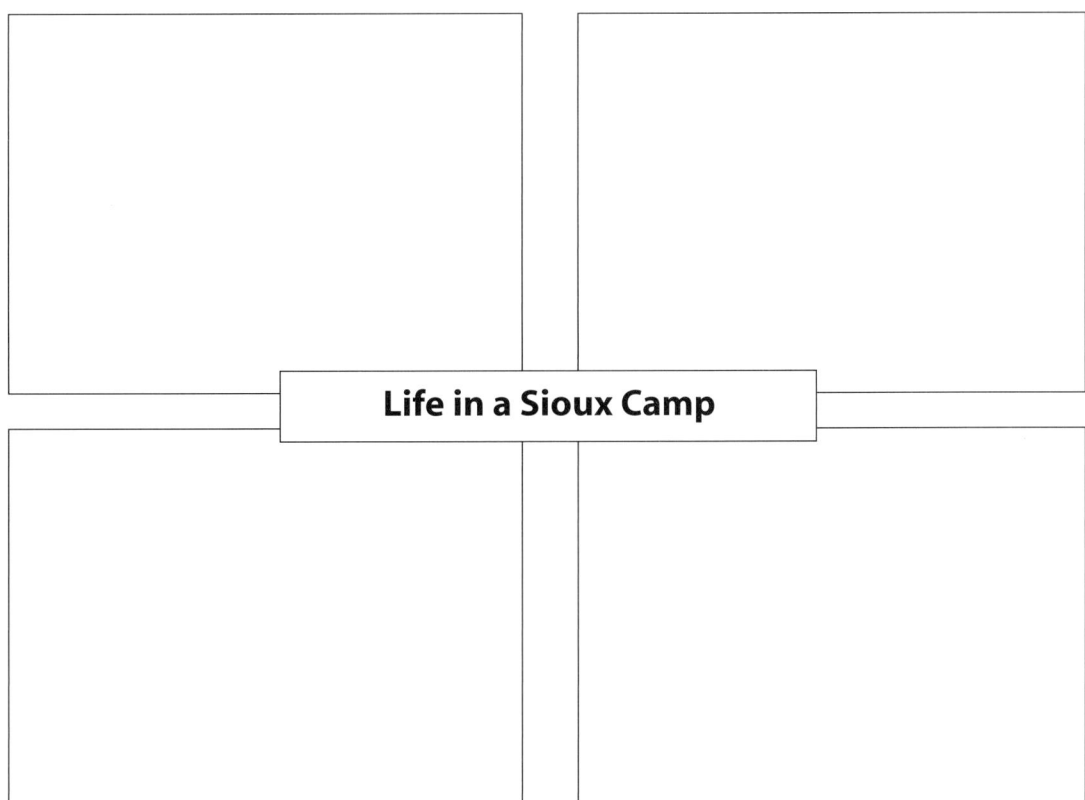

Activity sheet – Native American Customs

Sioux children

☞ Imagine that you are a child in a Sioux Indian camp. Use the information from the Resource sheets, 'What was daily life like for a Sioux Indian' and 'Nippiwan's diary, (part one) and (part two)', to write a diary extract as if you were a Sioux Indian child. Use the writing frame below to help you.

Dear diary,

Activity sheet – Native American Customs

History bingo

Your teacher will read out a list of keywords you have just learned from this unit, which you will then place on your bingo sheet. Your teacher will then read out a list of definitions. If you think you have the keyword to match, cross it off your list. If you complete a line, shout 'Bingo' and explain the meaning of the words you have to your teacher.

Assessment sheet – Native American Customs

✓ Tick the boxes to show what you know.

I know:

	Yes	Not sure	Don't know
who sat on the Sioux Council			
what punishments children were given			
what 'polygamy' means			
what 'exposure' means			
how to select information			
how to write a diary extract			
how to use keywords appropriately			

The thing that I remember the most about this unit is:

_____

_____

_____

_____

_____

Teacher's notes

The Buffalo

Objectives

- To understand how important the buffalo was to the Sioux Indians
- To use picture sources to correctly select information useful for answering questions
- To complete a piece of empathetic writing

Prior knowledge

Students will be aware of the Sioux's dependence upon the buffalo for food from previous units. This unit will examine this concept in more depth.

QCA and NC links

Consider the significance of events, people and developments in their historical context and in the present day.
Identify and investigate, individually and as part of a team, specific historical questions or issues, making and testing hypotheses.

Northern Ireland PoS

Describe and explain important historical concepts associated with the periods studied.
Assess the significance of the main events, people and changes studied.

Scottish attainment targets

Describe some features of events and so on from the past and suggest why they might be considered significant.

Background

The Sioux Indians had a nomadic existence, which mainly consisted of moving camp three times a year in order to follow the wandering buffalo across the Great Plains. The buffalo was more than a food source to the Sioux Indians and every part of the buffalo was used by them, for example, the hide was used as carpet, clothes and bedspreads. Without the buffalo the Sioux Indians would have died. They never killed more buffalo than they needed.

Starter activity

Ask students to suggest different ways in which their family can get food to eat and other items that they may need. Use this as a hook to get the students interested in how people survived before shops were around. Use, 'A world before shops', to help you.

Resource sheets and Activity sheets

Students will use the starter Activity sheet, 'A world before shops', to brainstorm about the different ways that they can get food and other goods today.

The Activity sheet,' The buffalo hunt', will provide students with an overview of a Sioux buffalo hunt on the Great Plains and will then encourage them to use the information that they have learned to answer some comprehension style tasks.

The Resource sheet, 'The buffalo', lets students look at the physical shape of a buffalo and what each part was called. This will be used in a future task. As well as this sheet, students can use the Resource sheet, 'What was the buffalo used for?', to identify each part of the buffalo and their uses.

The Activity sheet, 'One-stop shop', is a sheet that requires students to have read through the two previous sheets and then use the information that they have acquired to complete some information-based tasks.

Plenary

Students can be 'hot seated' as a Sioux warrior who has just taken part in a buffalo hunt. Try and draw out from them details from the information provided in this unit.

Assessment sheet

Students should complete an assessment sheet that will allow them to discover exactly what they have learned and can remember from this unit.

Activity sheet – The Buffalo

A world before shops

☞ Use this sheet to draw as many ways that you can get food and other goods for your family today. Be as creative as you can and do not just think of going to shops.

| **Goods for my family** |

Activity sheet – The Buffalo

The buffalo hunt

Buffalos were usually 1.5 metres tall. They ran quickly and any person that got in their way could find themselves crushed to death. Sioux hunters had to be very skilled or they would not eat.

A successful hunt would see the hunters surrounding a herd of buffalo on the Great Plains. The Sioux were so skilled that they could kill enough buffalos to provide the camp with food and tools in about 15 minutes.

A buffalo hunt was always noisy and extremely dangerous. The main reason for this was because the hunt confused the animals and they then ran around in a circle of panic trying to get away.

There were lots of techniques for killing a buffalo. Some hunters wore the skin of a buffalo and crept up behind their prey with a spear. Some rode on horseback and speared buffalo that way.

If on horseback, the Sioux hunter would ride as close to the back of the buffalo herd as possible, until he had selected the buffalo that he had chosen to kill. He would then try to separate the animal that he had chosen from the herd as soon as he could. The hunter did this by putting his horse between the animal that he had selected and the rest of the herd, forcing it to run off by itself. The hunter would then kill it without the danger of being trampled to death.

The buffalo was then dragged back to camp and the hunter's wife, or wives, would remove the skin, cook the meat and use the rest of the animal to make whatever tools and clothes were needed.

Task:

☞ Use the information on this sheet to answer some comprehension questions below. Use a separate piece of paper for your answers.

1. How tall were buffalos?
2. How long did it take a skilled group of hunters to kill a herd of buffalos?
3. Explain two ways that a hunter could attack a buffalo.

Resource sheet – The Buffalo

The buffalo

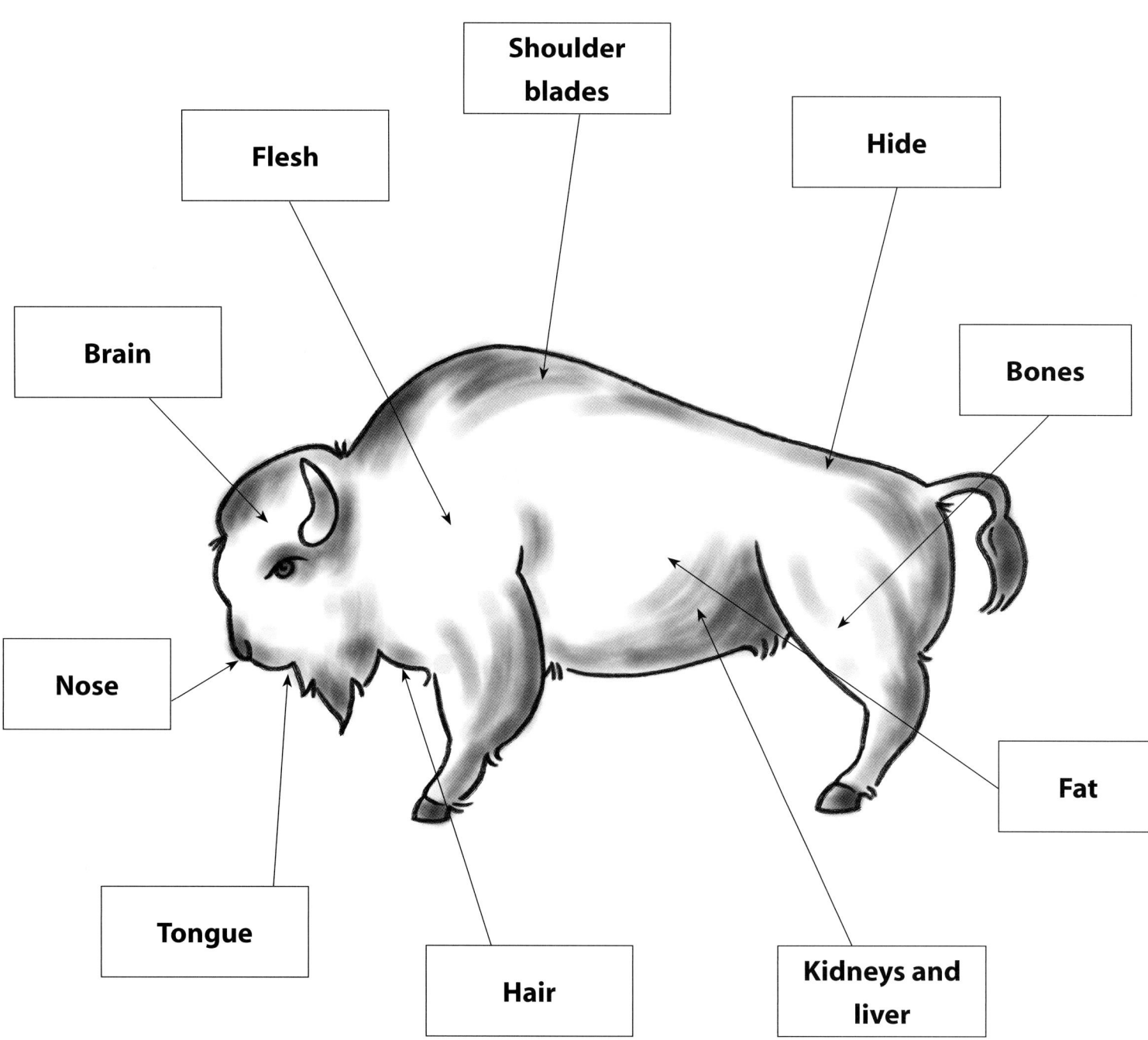

Resource sheet – The Buffalo

What was the buffalo used for?

The Sioux Indians could not go to a local shop to buy food. They could not buy clothes and they had to make all of the tools that they used to hunt, cook and make clothes with.

The buffalo was their 'one-stop shop'. They used every part of the buffalo and nothing went to waste. Have a look at the boxes below to see what the buffalo was used for.

Food

Buffalo meat and organs were eaten by the Sioux Indians.

1   They would roast, boil and dry smoke the meat.
2   They would eat raw brain, tongue and nose.
3   They would eat raw liver and kidneys.

Clothes and tepees

Buffalo skin was taken off the animal and used by the Indians.

1   It was used for tepees, clothes, shoes, warrior shields, a knife sheath and to make quivers for arrows.

Tools

The Sioux Indians used parts of the buffalo to make tools they needed.

1   The shoulder blade bones were used to make farming tools.
2   Hair was used to make rope and pillows.
3   Buffalo fat was turned into soap.
4   Bones and horns became paint brushes, knives and weapons.
5   The tongue was sometimes used as a hairbrush.

Activity sheet – The Buffalo

One-stop shop

Use all of the information from the last two sheets to complete the tasks below.

☞ 1 Use the two Resource sheets, 'The buffalo', and the, 'What was the buffalo used for?', to label and explain each part of the buffalo in the boxes on the diagram below. One has already been done for you.

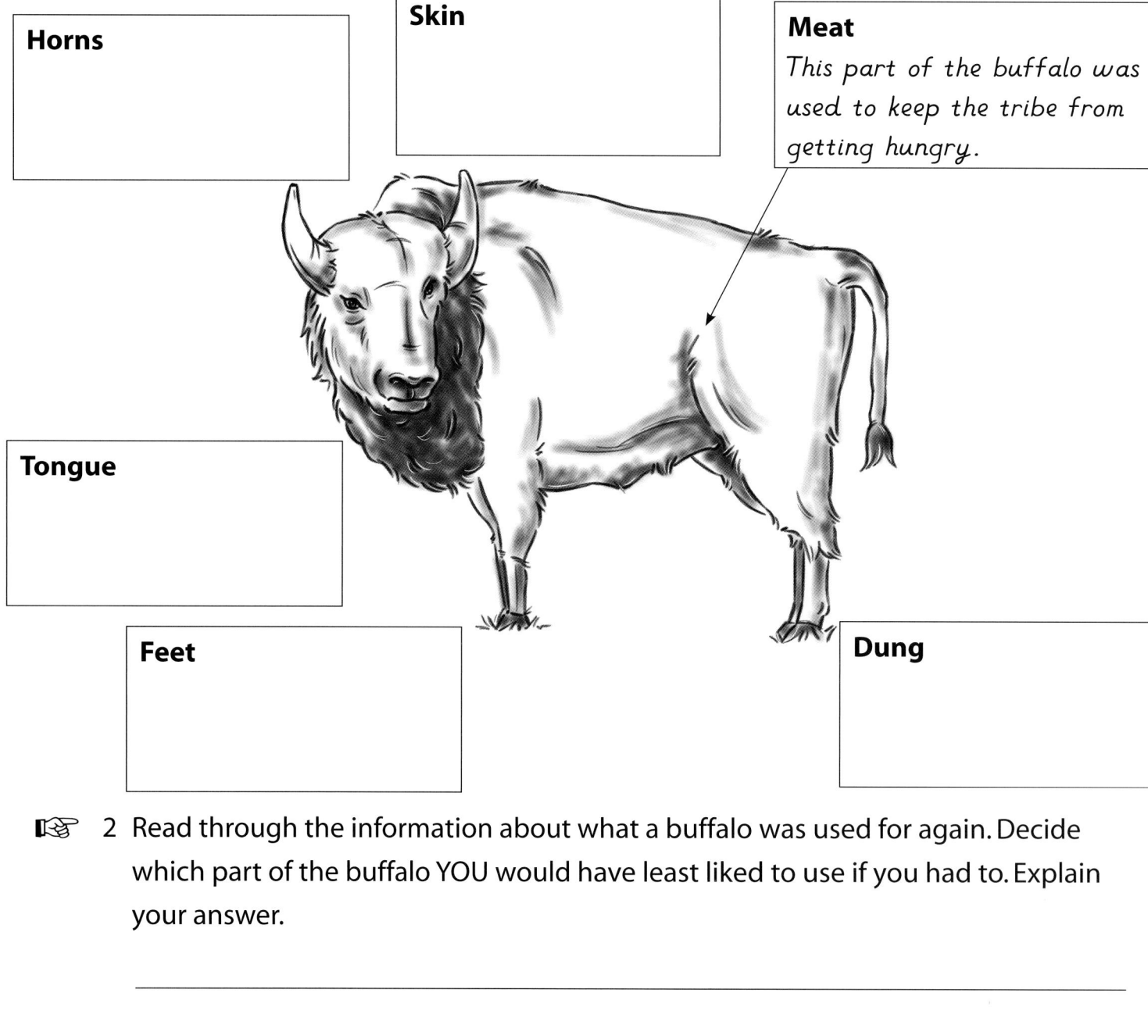

Horns

Skin

Meat
This part of the buffalo was used to keep the tribe from getting hungry.

Tongue

Feet

Dung

☞ 2 Read through the information about what a buffalo was used for again. Decide which part of the buffalo YOU would have least liked to use if you had to. Explain your answer.

_____
_____
_____
_____

Assessment sheet – The Buffalo

Use this sheet to see how much you can remember about the buffalo.

✓ Tick the ones that are true.

✗ Cross the ones that are false.

	The buffalo was hunted by a tank.

The buffalo was 3 metres tall.	

	The hunter would use either a spear or a bow and arrow to kill the buffalo.

Hunting the buffalo was an easy job and people never died.	

	The buffalo was used for meat, clothes and tools.

The tongue of a buffalo was used as a hairbrush.	

All of the meat on a buffalo was eaten after it had been cooked.	

Teacher's notes

Marriage and Divorce

Objectives

- To understand that not all religions and cultures have the same ideas about marriage
- To appreciate how a Sioux marriage was divorced
- To develop writing skills by using a writing frame

Prior knowledge

Students will have briefly touched upon family life and marriage in Unit 2. This unit will expand upon the concepts of marriage, polygamy and divorce in a Sioux tribe.

QCA and NC links

Understand the diverse experiences and ideas, beliefs and attitudes of men, women and children in past societies and how these have shaped the world.
Analyse and explain the reasons for, and results of, historical events, situations and changes.

Northern Ireland PoS

Identify and analyse the characteristic features of periods and societies studied.
Describe and explain reasons for and results of some of the historical events and changes in the periods studied.

Scottish attainment targets

Describe the diversity of lifestyles of people in the past.
Give some reasons to explain why a specific historical event and so on took place and the consequences.

Background

Family life was very important to the Sioux Indians. There was a great emphasis on getting married and having children. Due to the dangerous buffalo hunting and fighting battles with tribe enemies it meant that there were always more women than men in the camp. It was acceptable for men to take more than one wife – this was called polygamy. A man was allowed to have more wives if he was a successful hunter and needed them to clean his buffalo skins.

Starter activity

Write a sentence based on this unit on the whiteboard. Give students five minutes to use the letters in the sentence to create as many words as they can linked to the Native American topic.

Resource sheets and Activity sheets

In the Activity sheet, 'Why do we get married?', students are given the opportunity to make sure that they know the different reasons why people get married in Great Britain today.

The Resource sheet, 'Sioux marriages', is an information sheet that outlines the key details of a Sioux marriage for students. It explains how a Sioux Indian became ready for marriage and how he courted his potential wife.

The Resource sheet, 'Polygamy', outlines the key details of polygamy for students. This is a sensitive topic and one which students like to debate, so it will require strict control over the classroom.

In the Activity sheet, 'Polygamous marriage', students use information from the previous sheet to complete tasks based upon the concept of polygamy and the reasons why Sioux tribes used this type of marriage.

In the Activity sheet, 'Sioux divorce', students will study information about the divorce process in a Sioux marriage and then use a writing frame to complete a short report.

Plenary

Students can have a class discussion on whether they think that monogamy or polygamy is a better method of marriage.

Assessment sheet

Students should complete an assessment sheet that will allow them to discover exactly what they have learned and can remember from this unit.

Activity sheet – Marriage and Divorce

Why do we get married?

Marriages take place in Great Britain every day. Most people get married because they are in love but some people get married for other reasons.

☞ In the boxes on the left, write the possible reasons why you think somebody might have got married. Write a number (between 1 and 5) next to each of your reasons, 1 being the most important reason and 5 being the least important.

Resource sheet – Marriage and Divorce

Sioux marriages

In order for a Sioux man to, marry the woman that he wanted to, he had to prove that he had killed an enemy or another person.

If a man demonstrated that he had killed an enemy he had to 'date' his future wife for three months before he was allowed to marry her.

If, at the end of three months, the woman's father liked the warrior, then he was allowed to marry the woman – so long as he brought the father a weapon such as a bow and arrow or a gun.

Once a Sioux man and woman were married they lived together and had children. Family life was very important to the Sioux.

Many Sioux warriors died in battle or by hunting buffalo. This meant that there were always more women than men in a Sioux camp. A woman was not allowed to stay single, so it was not unusual for a man to have more than one wife.

This was called **POLYGAMY**.

Resource sheet – Marriage and Divorce

Polygamy

Sioux Indians did not have money. A Sioux warrior who was a very successful hunter was considered to be very wealthy. The more wealth that a warrior had, the more wives he was allowed to have.

A man could only have more than one wife if he killed enough buffalo to feed and clothe them. Every buffalo needed to be skinned and the more wives a man had, the more work could be completed. More wives meant that the work of skinning a buffalo and looking after the children was shared.

If a man was killed in battle or during a buffalo hunt then his brother was expected to marry his brother's wife and feed and clothe their children.

This system of marriage was called polygamy. Polygamy is when a man has more than one wife. It may seem strange to people today that a man can have more than one wife but the Sioux Indians saw it as the best solution for making sure that every woman had a husband and was provided for. Wives could share the work and everybody in the tribe was looked after.

Activity sheet – Marriage and Divorce

Polygamous marriage

Polygamous marriage was a great way to make sure that everybody in the Sioux tribe was looked after. The diagram below shows the different reasons why polygamy was used.

Why was polygamy a good idea?

A Sioux warrior had to marry his brother's wife if he was killed in battle.

 1 Look at the diagram above and then write the correct sentence from the following list in the space next to the matching picture. One has already been done for you.

　a It made it easier to clean the buffalo skins if there were more people to do the work.
　b A warrior could have lots of wives if he killed many buffalos.
　c ~~A Sioux warrior had to marry his brother's wife if he was killed in battle.~~
　d There were more women than men because so many warriors died in battle.

 2 On a separate sheet of paper, explain which reason for polygamy you think was the best.

Activity sheet – Marriage and Divorce

Sioux divorce

A wife was treated very well in a Sioux marriage. The main reason she was treated so well was because whilst her husband hunted, she did all of the hard work:

- Cooking
- Cleaning
- Putting up the tepee
- Packing up the tepee
- Cleaning the buffalo skins
- Making tools
- Making clothes
- Educating the children

If a marriage was not working it was easy for both men and women to get a divorce. A husband would bang a drum in the middle of the camp, which told the tribe that he was divorcing his wife. A wife would just move all of her belongings back to her parent's tepee.

☞ Imagine that you are writing a report for school on Sioux Indian divorce. Use the writing frame below to structure your report properly.

The reason why a wife was treated well was because _____

_____

_____

It was easy for a husband to divorce his wife because _____

_____

_____

It is easy for a wife to divorce her husband because _____

_____

_____

© Folens (copiable page)   Native American Indians

Assessment sheet – Marriage and Divorce

✓ Tick the boxes that show what you know.

I know:

	Yes	Not Sure	Don't Know
what 'marriage' means			
what a divorce is			
what 'polygamy' means			
how Sioux Indians got divorced			
what a writing frame is			
how to use written information			
how to give detailed reasons			

The thing that I remember the most about this unit is:

_____

_____

_____

_____

_____

Teacher's notes

Native American Beliefs

Objectives

- To develop an understanding of what the Great Spirit was
- To utilise information to complete comprehension tasks
- To learn the meaning of keywords via 'History Pictionary'

Prior knowledge

Students will need to know what the word 'religion' means. It can be linked in a cross-curricular way with RS as this lesson will study the religious beliefs of the Sioux tribe.

QCA and NC links

Understand the diverse experiences and ideas, beliefs and attitudes of men, women, and children in past societies and how these have shaped the world.

Northern Ireland PoS

Identify and analyse the characteristic features of periods and societies studied.

Scottish attainment targets

Describe the diversity of lifestyles of people in the past.

Resource sheets and Activity sheets

In the Resource sheet, 'What was the Great Spirit?', teacher and students can read about the Sioux concept of the Great Spirit. Then there is a short task asking students to explain, in their own words, what they think 'Great Spirit' means.

The Resource sheet, 'Sioux Religion', provides students with information about the religious beliefs that the Sioux Indians had.

'Wakan Tanka', is an Activity sheet that asks students to write a prayer to their God, Wakan Tanka, using the template provided.

The Resource sheet, 'The Medicine Man', is an information sheet which provides students with information about the role of the Medicine Man. It will be vital for the Activity sheet, 'Medicine Man advert', which asks students to design an advertisement for a Medicine Man on the template provided.

Plenary

Play a game of History Pictionary using some of the keywords learned so far.

Assessment sheet

Students should complete a true or false activity to assess what they have learned during this unit of the textbook.

Background

The Sioux Indians did not worship a religion in the same way that many people do today. They believed that everything had a spirit and that the world would work in harmony. They believed that a Great Spirit had created them and everything in the world around them. This influenced the way that they lived and hunted the buffalo.

Starter activity

Write the word 'religion' on the board and get the class to brainstorm about what they think the word means and all of the different ways that people can worship a religion today.

Resource sheet – Native American Beliefs

What was the Great Spirit?

The Sioux Indians who lived on the Great Plains in America tried to live in harmony with nature. They made sure that they did very little damage to the environment that they lived in. This was very important as they relied upon the grassland and wildlife to keep them alive.

The most important part of the Sioux beliefs was the Great Spirit. They believed that the Great Spirit controlled every part of their lives from hunting to the weather.

What did the Indians believe about the Great Spirit?

- The Great Spirit would help hunters to be successful.
- The Great Spirit would provide good or bad weather.
- The phrase 'GreatSpirit' means 'Great Mystery'. They sometimes called him Wakan Tanka.
- The Sioux believed that the Great Spirit had given every living thing a spirit to worship.
- The Great Spirit would look at how people behaved on earth and send them to a suitable place when they died.

☞ On a separate piece of paper explain what the Sioux Indians believed about the Great Spirit in your own words.

Resource sheet – Native American Beliefs

Sioux religion

How did the Sioux Indians view the world around them?

The Sioux Indians believed in living in harmony with the spirits of every living thing around them. They felt that there were religious spirits all around them that could bring good or evil harmony to their camp and tribe. They kept a close eye on nature because changes might suggest disruption among the spirits, for example, if a river had deep swirling currents then it was a sign that evil spirits were nearby.

Unlike the white settlers who would later settle on the Great Plains, the Sioux Indians only killed enough animals to feed and clothe themselves. They believed that wasting any part of the buffalo was an insult to their Great Spirit. The Sioux Indians spent their entire lives praying, offering sacrifices and holding daily ceremonies. This was all meant to keep the spirits happy and show thanks to their Great Spirit.

Activity sheet – Native American Beliefs

Wakan Tanka

☞ Imagine that you are writing a prayer to the Great Spirit. Use the template below to write your prayer. It must explain what you hope to gain from the prayer and what you will do in return for having good crops or a great hunt!

Oh Great Wakan Tanka,

Resource sheet – Native American Beliefs

The Medicine Man

In every Sioux tribe there was one person who was best at contacting the Great Spirit. This person would be the Medicine Man. The only person more important than the Medicine Man was the Chief.

The Medicine Man performed all of the special ceremonies in a Sioux camp. The members of the tribe believed that a Medicine Man had magical powers. Usually this person was a man but occasionally a married woman could become one if she showed magical powers.

The Medicine Man was expected to do many things that would help his tribe:

- predict the future;
- advise the tribe about fighting battles;
- cast love spells for married couples;
- heal the sick and wounded after battles;
- protect the tribe from evil spirits.

Medicine Men explained natural events such as thunderstorms as being signs from the Great Spirit. They also used many techniques to try and contact the Great Spirit. They chanted, played music and sometimes mixed herbs together to try and fall into a trance. This trance-like state was when people felt that they left their bodies and contacted the spirits.

The Medicine Man also helped people when they became ill by using the plants and herbs that they could find around them. They developed a very good knowledge of plants that grew on the Great Plains and knew which ones could cure illnesses.

Activity sheet – Native American Beliefs

Medicine Man advert

☞ Imagine that you have to write an advertisement to find a Medicine Man for your tribe. Use the space below to design your advert.

Remember, make it colourful and say what talents a Medicine Man should have.

Assessment sheet – Native American Beliefs

Use this sheet to see how much you can remember about Native American beliefs.

✓ Tick the ones that are true.

✗ Cross the ones that are false.

	The Sioux Indians believed in the Great Spirit.

All Medicine Men were male.	

	The Sioux Indians believed that the Great Spirit influenced everything that happened to them.

The Medicine Man was meant to protect the tribe from evil spirits.	

	The Medicine Man used drugs to go into a trance.

Another name for the Great Spirit was Wakan Tanka.	

	A trance-like state can be when people feel that they leave their bodies and contact the spirits.

Teacher's notes

Native American Warfare

Objectives
- To select and use information correctly
- To use information to plan a historical battle

Prior knowledge
Students need to be made aware that there as more than one tribe of Native American Indians living on the Great Plains and that there were often battles between these tribes.

QCA and NC links
Present and organise accounts and explanations about the past that are coherent, structured and substantiated, using chronological conventions historical vocabulary.
Identify and investigate, individually and as part of a team, specific historical questions or issues, making and testing hypotheses.

Northern Ireland PoS
Describe and explain important historical concepts associated with the periods studied.
Recall, select and organise information deploying terms accurately to communicate their knowledge and understanding of history.

Scottish attainment targets
Describe the diversity of lifestyles of people in the past.

Resource sheets and Activity sheets
The Resource sheet, 'Why did Sioux Indians fight?', explains to students the different reasons why Plains Indians chose to go into battle with the enemy. There are comprehension questions at the bottom of the sheet.

The Resource sheet, 'Bravery in battle', introduces students to the various actions that could take place during battle, such as scalping and counting coup. This resource will be useful for the Activity sheet, 'Bravery in battle activities'. This activity sheet asks students to use the information from the previous sheet to complete an activity where they must fill in the gaps.

The Activity sheet, 'An account of a battle', asks students to use the information they have learned to devise the best battle plan that they possibly can for an Indian raid.

Plenary
Students will read out the battle plans that they wrote and their peers will assess them.

Assessment sheet
Students will complete an assessment sheet that will allow them to discover exactly what they have learnt and can remember from this unit.

Background
Sioux warriors were always expected to prove themselves in battle and they were often given the chance to do this. Sioux tribes would fight each other for pride and to steal horses from each other. A brave fighter could expect to have great wealth within the tribe and take many wives.

Starter activity
Students can brainstorm on the board as to what qualities would make a Sioux Indian a good warrior.

Activity sheet – Native American Warfare

Why did Sioux Indians fight?

The Sioux Indians followed the buffalo wherever they went, so lived a wandering lifestyle. This meant that the Sioux tribes did not own land of their own and never had to steal land off their enemies.

One of the main reasons that the Sioux went to war was over horses. The first horses were brought to America by white settlers. Some horses escaped and became wild. The Sioux decided to use these horses to hunt. A man who had a lot of horses was seen as a rich man. If a warrior wanted a good wife then he needed to own a lot of horses, so tribes stole horses from each other.

The Sioux Indians fought for four main reasons:
- To take human scalps from the enemy to prove their bravery.
- To make their tribe seem powerful.
- To steal horses from other tribes.
- To get revenge on their enemies.

The Sioux Indians were often keen to fight battles and wars with enemy tribes as it would give them a chance to win glory for their family. Sometimes a battle might start just because of one person seeking revenge on an enemy.

☞ Use the information above to complete the comprehension tasks below. Write your answers on a separate piece of paper.

1 What animal did the Sioux Indians follow?
2 Why did Sioux Indians not have to steal land from their enemies?
3 Explain four reasons why Sioux Indians went into battle.

Resource sheet – Native American Warfare

Bravery in battle

Sioux Indians were very brave and strong warriors. They were also very clever in battle. When planning an attack on the enemy, they would always use surprise and try to attack when the other tribe were not expecting them to.

A surprise raid on the enemy would give the Sioux Indians a better chance for bravery and cunning in battle. Most importantly, it lowered the chances of being killed.

A group of 20 to 30 Sioux warriors, who were sometimes known as 'braves', would attack their enemy and by using surprise it meant that only one or two of these braves would be killed.

Only Sioux men were allowed to fight in battle. Sioux women were expected to stay at home in the camp. Their job would be to look after the tribe's children and any wounded braves after battle.

The Indians considered bravery to be very important but they thought that dying in battle was stupid. A warrior could shoot an enemy with a bow and arrow but if a warrior wanted

to show how brave he really was in battle, he would get close enough to touch the enemy with a stick but not kill him. This was called counting coup. They had a special coup stick and everytime a warrior touched a man in battle with the stick they were allowed to put another feather on the stick!

Another way that a Sioux brave could show how brave he had been in battle was by collecting the scalps of his enemies. The Sioux believed that the spirit of the enemy killed in battle would haunt them if they did not take the scalp of their enemy.

Warriors would lift the dead brave's head up and use a sharp knife to cut off the skin from the top of his head. This would then be a prized trophy to the Sioux warrior. The more scalps a warrior had, the braver he was in battle.

When white settlers arrived in America, they were the most afraid of being scalped by the Plains Indians if they were caught in battle. Many white settlers felt that the Plains Indians were savages for scalping their enemies.

Activity sheet – Native American Warfare

Bravery in battle activities

Use the 'Bravery in battle' Resource sheet to complete the tasks below.

☞ 1 Complete the comprehension tasks below:

- What was another name for an Indian warrior?
  _____

- How did the Sioux warriors attack the enemy?
  _____

- Who was not allowed to fight in battles and what role did they play?
  _____

☞ 2 Fill in the passage below using blanks in the box below it:

The Sioux Indians would use a **c**_____ stick to touch his enemies in battle. This proved how **b**_____ he was. He would then put more **f**_____ on his stick to show how many people he had touched. The Sioux Indians would use a knife to **s**_____ their enemies. Scalping showed how **b**_____ they were in battle. To **s**_____ a man a Sioux Indian would sometimes use a very **s**_____ **k**_____ and cut off scalp off his enemies **h**_____. An enemies **s**_____ was a prized trophy amongst the **P**_____ Indians. Many white **p**_____ were very scared of the Sioux warrior. They believed that the Plains Indians were **s**_____ and should be **k**_____ to stop them from killing white people.

sharp	**s**calp	**k**nife	**f**eathers	
scalp	**h**ead	**p**eople	**b**rave	**s**avages	**P**lains
brave		**k**illed		**s**calp	**c**oup

Native American Indians 49

Activity sheet – Native American Warfare

An account of a battle

You have read about how the Sioux warriors fought their battles and what they did to their enemy during battle. Imagine that you are a white settler watching a battle.

☞ Describe what you see, feel, hear and smell on the notepad below.

Assessment sheet – Native American Warfare

✓ Tick the boxes to show what you know.

I know:

	Yes	Not Sure	Don't Know
what 'counting coup' means			
what 'scalping' means			
how important horses were to the Indians			
what role men and women played in battle			
how to select information			
how to answer comprehension questions			

The thing that I remember the most about this unit is:

_____

_____

_____

_____

Teacher's notes

Problems with White Settlers

Objectives

- To extract historical information from a written source
- To understand what problems arose with the arrival of white settlers
- To develop discussion skills

Prior knowledge

Students will need to be aware of the fact that white settlers arrived in America from Europe during the 17th century and eventually began to spread out towards the Great Plains. This clashed with the Sioux way of life.

QCA and NC links

Analyse and explain the reasons for, and results of, historical events, situations and changes.
Present and organise accounts and explanations about that are coherent, structured and substantiated, using chronological conventions and historical vocabulary.

Northern Ireland PoS

Describe and explain reasons for and results of some of the historical events and changes in the periods studied.
Recall, select and organise information deploying terms accurately to communicate their knowledge and understanding of history.

Scottish attainment targets

Give some reasons to explain why a specific historical event and so on took place and the consequences.

Starter activity

Students should discuss the problems that they think might arise for the Sioux Indians from the arrival of white settlers on the Great Plains.

Resource sheets and Activity sheets

The Resource sheet, 'Settlers arrive', outlines the arrival of white settlers in America.
    The Resource sheet, 'Settlers arrive source sheet', is a simple information sheet continuing the explanation of the different ways in which the settlers changed the Sioux Indians' lives.
    Students should use the Resource sheets to undertake a chart filling activity on the Activity sheet, 'Settlers arrive worksheet', explaining the effects of the white settlers.
    Students will need to use all the Resource sheets and previous Activity sheets in this unit to write a short essay about the conflict between white settlers and Sioux Indians.

Plenary

Students can design their own wordsearch based upon the words used in this unit.

Assessment sheet

Students should complete a true or false activity to assess what they have learned during this unit of the textbook.

Background

The major problem when the white settlers arrived in America from Europe was that they wanted to spread out across the country. This meant that many white settlers wanted to settle on the Great Plains and use the buffalo as a food supply. There were great clashes between the Plains Indians and new arrivals as they did not speak the same language or have the same cultures.

Resource sheet – Problems with White Settlers

Settlers arrive

White settlers who arrived in America in the 18th century soon travelled further inland from the coast. They built towns and cities but it became clear that new places were needed for people to live in.

Settlers started to look at the Great Plains of America as a good place to live. The Plains Indians welcomed new settlers at first because they thought that everybody should share the land that the Great Spirit had given them.

There were obvious problems such as the fact that Plains Indians and the settlers could not speak the same language and they had very different cultures. It did not take long for conflict to begin.

Problems between white settlers and Plains Indians

© Folens (copiable page)   Native American Indians

Resource sheet – Problems with White Settlers

Settlers arrive source sheet

It became clear that white settlers and Sioux Indians could not live on the same land together.

- The Sioux Indians relied upon the buffalo for food, clothing and tools. They never killed more than they needed but the white settlers killed more buffalos than they could eat.
- White settlers were used to common colds but for the Sioux Indians, who had never had a cold before, these were very dangerous and could even cause death.
- The Sioux Indians lived at one with the land but the white settlers dug it up and built roads and houses. The Sioux Indians thought that the settlers would upset the Great Spirit with the way that they treated the land.
- White settlers were looking for gold. This would make them rich and many gold mines were built on land where the Sioux Indians camped. The settlers tried to make the Native Americans leave their land.

Source 1 – Diary Extract – Louise Mercer – 1867

'I can remember the first time we met with the Indians. My husband, Kirby, had a cold and he couldn't stop sneezing. The Chief laughed at first but a week later my daughter, Charlotte, told me that many of the tribe were sick and some had even died.'

Source 2 – History Textbook – Jemma Baker

Historians believe that the tribe that suffered most from new diseases brought by white people were the Mandans. They had a tribe of 1600 people but only 31 survived a smallpox outbreak in 1837.

Source 3 – Rev. K. Moore – 1855

As we were ploughing, mining and building our new towns on the Great Plains, we could see the Indians watching us on the hills. They looked shocked at what we were doing to the land.

Source 4 – Newspaper Extract – E. Ord – 1860

The United States government urges all white settlers to kill as many buffalo as they can. They ask that you do this so that the Indians become weak and give up their land to the government for you to build on and farm.

Activity sheet – Problems with White Settlers

Settlers arrive worksheet

☞ Use the information on the last two sheets to complete the chart below. Fill in as much detail as you can in the relevant sections of the chart.

Problems with buffalo	**Problems with diseases**

Problems with land	**Problems with weapons**

Activity sheet – Problems with White Settlers

Settlers arrive essay task

In your own words, explain the different effects that the arrival of white settlers had on the Plains Indians. You should write about at least four changes that affected the Sioux Indians. Use the chart on the previous sheet to help you.

Assessment sheet – Problems with White Settlers

Use this sheet to see how much you can remember about the arrival of white settlers in America.

| ✓ | Tick the ones that are true. |
| X | Cross the ones that are false. |

| | **The white settlers caused no problems when they arrived.** |

| **The Plains Indians caught no diseases from the settlers.** | |

| | **The Plains Indians traded food for clothing.** |

| **The settlers were looking for gold to mine.** | |

| | **The settlers only killed the number of buffalo that they needed.** |

| **The Plains Indians were upset that settlers were not respecting the land.** | |

| | **The government asked the settlers to stop killing buffalo.** |

Teacher's notes

Battle of Little Big Horn

Objectives
- To understand what interpretation means
- To use evidence to answer questions
- To undertake discussion activities

Prior knowledge
Students will be aware of how unhappy the Plains Indians were with the arrival of the white settlers and how their lives were changed by them. This would ultimately lead to serious problems between the two groups.

QCA and NC links
Understand how historians and others form interpretations.
Present and organise accounts and explanations about the past that are coherent, structured and substantiated, using chronological conventions and historical vocabulary.

Northern Ireland PoS
Consider how and why some historical events, people and changes have been interpreted differently.
Recall, select and organise information deploying terms accurately to communicate their knowledge and understanding of history.

Scottish attainment targets
Describe the diversity of lifestyles of people in the past.

Starter activity
Students should look at the pictures of an American soldier and a Plains Indian warrior on, 'Who would win?'. They should discuss which one they feel would be more successful in a battle.

Resource sheets and Activity sheets
The Resource sheet, 'Who would win?', asks students to decide which soldier would be more likely to win in a battle against each other – an army soldier or a Sioux warrior.

The two Resource sheets, 'The Battle of Little Big Horn (1)' and '(2)', explain what led to the Battle of Little Big Horn and how the events played out. The information will be useful for the next two activities.

The Activity sheet, 'Warrior Diary', encourages the students to write a diary account of a warrior who took part in the Battle of Little Big Horn.

The Activity sheet, 'Newspaper report', asks students to use the previous sheets to help write a newspaper report that explains how the white settlers felt about the Battle of Little Big Horn and the death of Lieutenant General George Custer.

Assessment sheet
Students should complete an assessment sheet that will allow them to discover exactly what they have learned and can remember from this unit.

Background

By 1876, the conflict between the Plains Indians and the white settlers had reached its most serious with the Battle of Little Big Horn. This was the worst battle between the two groups and despite the fact that the Indians won the battle, it would ultimately lead to the breakdown of the Plains Indians.

Resource sheet – Battle of Little Big Horn

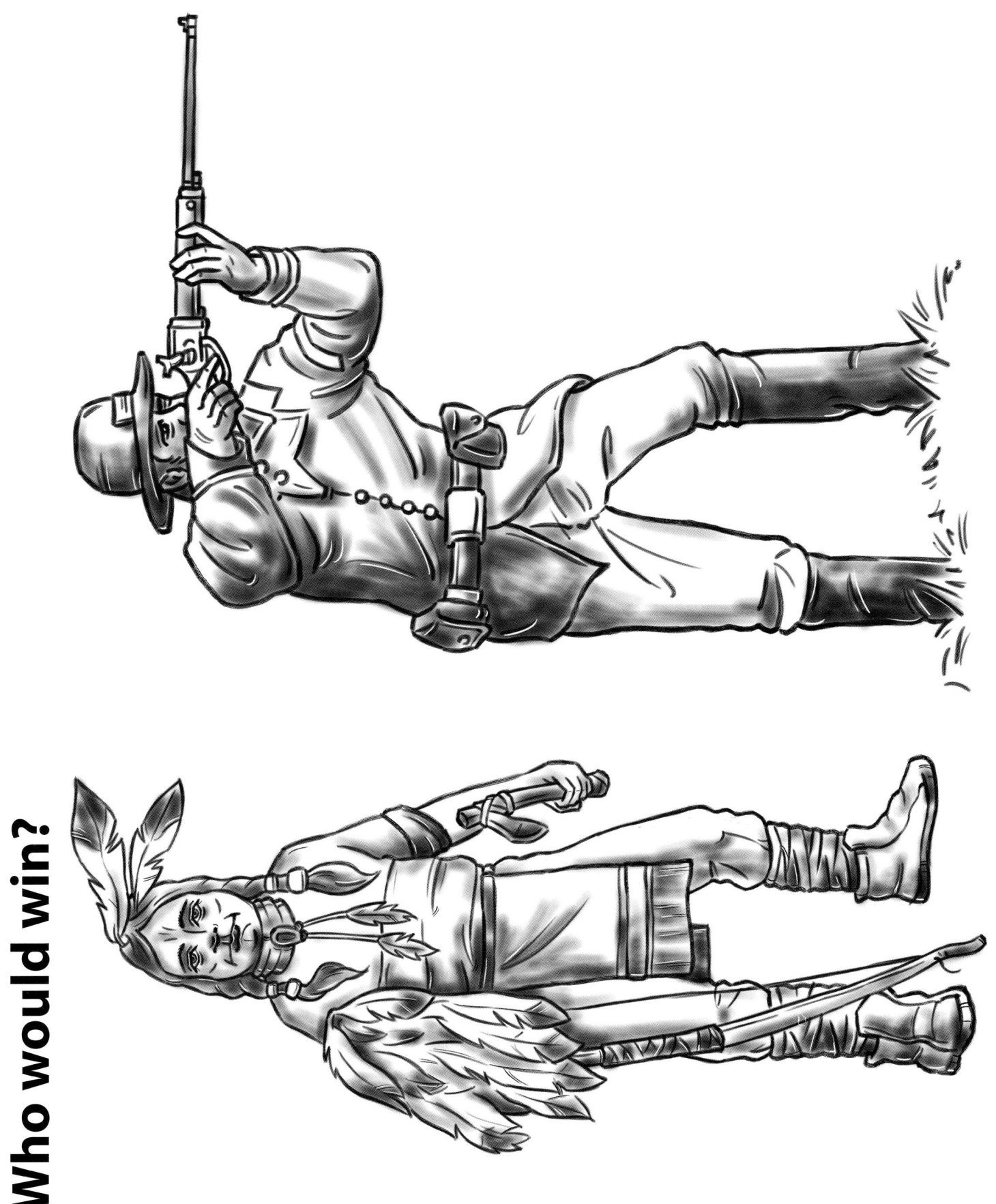

Who would win?

Resource sheet – Battle of Little Big Horn

Battle of Little Big Horn (1)

By 1850, the US government was forcing tribes to live in large areas of land called reservations. The rest of the land was given to white settlers. The Native American tribes were unhappy about this. They believed that nobody owned land, so it was not right for the government to decide where the Plains Indians could live.

The disagreements between the Plains Indians and the white settlers became worse in 1875. The government had promised an Indian Chief called Red Cloud that no white settlers would live in the Black Hills. This was a sacred area for the Sioux Indians but the settlers discovered gold there and ignored the Fort Laramie Treaty that stated they could not live there.

The Sioux Indians were so angry that they gathered to defend their sacred land. They were led by a man called Chief Sitting Bull.

The government panicked and sent the Army to force the Sioux Indians back to their reservation. The Seventh Cavalry was led by a man called Lieutenant Colonel George Custer. Custer noticed that there was a Sioux village just 15 miles from where the Sioux army had gathered. Custer wanted to attack the village but was ordered to wait by the army officer above him.

Custer ignored these orders. What Custer did not know is that the number of warriors in the Sioux village was three times the size of the Seventh Cavalry.

Custer's plan was simple. He split his troops into three groups. He sent the first group of soldiers to the Little Big Horn River. They were meant to stop the warriors escaping when the village was attacked.

Custer then ordered another group of soldiers to attack the village. The third group of soldiers would follow behind and kill any warriors that escaped.

The plan failed.

Resource sheet – Battle of Little Big Horn

Battle of Little Big Horn (2)

A group of Sioux and Cheyenne warriors crossed the river first and attacked the soldiers advancing on the village. This forced Custer's soldiers backwards. They were split off from their support on the other side of the village.

Another Native American, called Crazy Horse, led a group of Oglala Sioux to attack Custer's men from behind. The Seventh Cavalry found themselves attacked on both sides with bow and arrows.

Custer had no way to protect his men so he ordered them to shoot their own horses and then stack the dead bodies around them to try and create a wall. He hoped that this would give them some protection from the attacking warriors.

Custer and his troop of men did not last an hour. The two groups that had separated from Custer managed to escape and join up. They waited for reinforcements to arrive. This defeat became known as 'Custer's Last Stand'. Every single man was killed by the Indian warriors. This was the worst American military disaster in history.

The defeat at Little Big Horn scared the US government and convinced them that revenge was needed. Custer was a Civil War hero and people wanted revenge for his death. The Plains Indians believed that they had showed the white settlers that they would no longer be pushed around. However the Plains tribes could not survive the onslaught of government revenge. In a matter of months, the government had taken complete control of the Great Plains of America.

The disagreement over the Black Hills was ended when the government rewrote the Fort Laramie Treaty and placed the sacred Black Hills land outside of the Plains Indians' reservation. This meant that white people could now settle there.

Just a year later, the Sioux Indians had been completely defeated and they could no longer defend themselves against white settlement of the Great Plains and their sacred land.

Activity sheet – Battle of Little Big Horn

Warrior diary

Imagine that you are a Sioux warrior who has taken part in the Battle of Little Big Horn. Use the diary writing frame below to explain what you did and how you felt about winning.

Dear diary,

_____
_____
_____
_____
_____
_____
_____
_____
_____
_____
_____
_____
_____

Activity sheet – Battle of Little Big Horn

Newspaper report

☞ Use the newspaper writing frame below to write an account about the Battle of Little Big Horn.

The North American Companion!
26th August 1876

LITTLE BIG HORN MASSACRE: CIVIL WAR HERO KILLED

Assessment sheet – Battle of Little Big Horn

✓ Tick the boxes to show what you know.

I know:

	Yes	**Not Sure**	**Don't Know**
who George Custer was			
what 'reservation' means			
what 'massacre' means			
who won the Battle of Little Big Horn			
about battles			
how to select information			
how to learn new words			

The thing that I remember the most about this unit is:

_____

_____

I need to work on (up to three targets):

1 _____

2 _____

3 _____